AF348581

ART AND ECONOMICS:

A Short History of Art Collecting

Charles Moore

Art and Economics: A Short History of Art Collecting NEW YORK, NEW YORK, U.S.A.

Published in the United States by Petite Ivy Press.

Library of Congress Control Number:
Names: MOORE, CHARLES, Author
Title: *Art and Economics: A Short History of Art Collecting* | CHARLES MOORE
Description: New York: Petite Ivy Press. [2024]
Identifiers: LCCN 2024938900(print) |
ISBN: 978-1-955496-12-4 (hardcover print)

Or perhaps it is only a record of that obscure mania which urges us as much to put together a collection as to keep a diary, in other words, the need to transform the flow of one's own existence into a series of objects, saved from dispersal, or into a series of written lines abstracted and crystallized from the continuous flux of thought.

—Italo Calvino, *Collection of Sand: Essays*

Collecting is the noblest of all passions!

—Wilhelm von Bode

CONTENTS

Chapter 1:
A Brief History of Consumerism: Between Vanity and *Vanitas*

In 1956, French philosopher Jean-Paul Sartre wrote that human beings are not made to be in the world as a "thing in a world of things." The existentialism current of thought explored the idea of freedom and absolute subjectivity as the essence of human beings (Dufrenne 1956). We are free to define ourselves as we prefer, regardless of our surroundings and objects. Human beings are free to exist according to their personal *existentialisms*, revolting against a system that objectifies and enslaves their subjectivity. However, contrary to Sartre's aspirations, we still live in an era in which our existence often depends on *things* outside of us. Identity, in a consumerist and capitalist age, often passes in its defining process through the possession of objects. And more and more, people tend to identify with the objects they buy and own—objects that are outside of themselves and yet that are able to represent them so much.

In particular, the consumption and possession of art intersect values strongly linked to collective consumption and social status and, at the same time, existentialist and individual self-worth. The identity of an art collector is formed through the possession of an object created by someone else that tells something strictly personal about them and their role in society. Collecting art means experiencing artistic culture essentially through the possession of art-objects. This possession of art-objects is in some cases guided by cultural motives, curiosity, erudition, devotion, or purely artistic interest; in other cases it is a speculative calculation, an economic investment, and even the urgent need for a prestigious social status, guided by self-affirmation, since works of art are never neutral consumer goods. Investigating the peculiar traits of art consumerism means observing the heterogeneity of human motives that drive the purchase behavior of a work of art. The important economic and socio-identity components of art collecting must be considered because they are intrinsic to the artistic object. Even at the base of collecting, in fact, there are objects. They are mythical objects, full of symbolic value, but they are still exemplary objects. Therefore, to understand art collecting, it is necessary to observe the work of art as a market category inserted into a broader theory of consumption.

In this chapter, we analyze how social stratification and identification in a particular social class influence the purchasing behavior of art collectors. We begin by briefly framing the consumerist attitude, starting from the assumption that it is not a necessarily negative, hedonistic, and materialistic human behavior but on the contrary a complex mix. Consumerism intersects individualistic and collective needs. Today more than ever, the relationship with objects, and in particular objects considered superfluous such as artworks, is charged with meanings that go beyond mere survival. However, this bond with the object and the impulse to buy it is not a novelty of the twenty-first century. Its history is rooted in past centuries, long before the advent of advertising and social media.

Consumerism evolved with the birth of discretionary income. Capital was available to invest in purchases that went beyond the mere necessities, which were already satisfied. Until the eighteenth century, people could afford only essential goods, but by the mid-eighteenth century in Europe, the economic expansion produced an increase in wages. This fact consequently created demand for new consumer goods: furniture, accessories, wigs, fancy clothes, and much more. This new disposable income sanctioned the birth of the modern leisure class, a social class that could afford and imagine a lifestyle surrounded by different objects. The consumerism we know today, the one characterized by mass production, planned obsolescence, and the continuous replacement of new objects, is the result of this historic moment of consumer and social class novelty. Even in the past, consumerism was steeped in contradictions. It was conceived as the enhancement of a virtuous business circle, but it was thought by others as morally unfair materialism. Which side was and is the reason?

Art history once again allows us to explore the complex dichotomous vision of this social and economic phenomenon. We can observe, for example, the art produced by the Dutch Republic of the seventeenth century. During this period, the nation was experiencing an incredible commercial expansion and a great growth of wealth. According to the scholar Honig (1998), it was a "mercantilist and proto-capitalist culture in which commodities played an immense role in the cultural consciousness." Art responded to this historic moment in which objects had extreme importance in society with the dizzying spread of the still life genre. Artists such as van Beyeren, Claesz, and de Heem created still life paintings of objects, flowers, food, and musical instruments with an almost maniacal obsession and the typical Flemish descriptivism. It is no coincidence;

the artists responded to the taste of an era and to the demands of a new bourgeois and mercantile social class that wanted to collect what it loved most: objects. At a time when "things were imported, things were crafted, things were traded" (Honig 1998), the pictorial representation of objects was a natural practice and soon spread throughout Europe. The subject of a still life, however, embodies interesting duplicity. The Dutch still life genre was also known as *vanitas*, a Latin word for vanity. The depicted goods were the symbol of wealth and status that only a small portion of the population could afford, fueling ego and vanity. But the word *vanitas* also has in its etymological root another implicit meaning. *Vanitas* derives from *vanus*, a term that means futile, empty, inconsistent, and especially ephemeral. This visual material obsession also embodies the consciousness of being surrounded by superfluous objects and, like wealth, is destined to perish, to be consumed. The theme of *vanitas* tells a lot about the consumerism of the time and ours. It expresses the point of view of a new capitalist society, where objects symbolized wealth, power, and fame but also hid a moralizing intention that warns about the consequences of excessive hedonism. The Dutch still life, therefore, oscillates between the "celebration of luxury and the condemnation" (Honig 1998) of it, and it highlights the subtle boundary between abundance and excess.

The example of *vanitas* in Dutch painting is functional in this discourse on the evolution of consumerism because it embodies the different visions toward the attachment to objects. A particularly original theoretical position was, for example, that of political economist Bernard Mandeville. In the first half of the eighteenth century, Mandeville published his controversial *Fable of the Bees*, an economic essay that supported a singular thesis: private vices, even superfluous purchases of the individual, have public benefits. According to scholars, the fable represents "the first presentation of the individualist conception of the natural economic order" (Chalk 1966)—private vices can produce a prosperous society. It was exactly the contrary of religion and moral conception. According to Mandeville, what made a nation rich and safe was a simple activity: shopping. It was not driven by vices, popularly considered immoral, but by passions that contributed to material prosperity. Mandeville challenged the ideas of vices and virtues, where only Christian, pauperist behavior could be considered right; he encouraged humans to "accept their natural selfishness" and stated that "people were hypocrites for espousing rigorous ideas about virtue and vice while they failed to act according to those beliefs in their private lives" (Chalk 1966).

Mandeville's point of view about society also introduced a new idea of the laissez-faire market, where economic affairs could be managed autonomously by individuals without government interference (Rosenberg 1963). *The Fable of the Bees*, a society where busy bees live in total virtue and honesty but without thinking about personal and collective gain, therefore doomed to failure, speaks of economics but above all of human nature. A human nature that, according to Mandeville, is intrinsically individualistic and selfish but that precisely through this push produces public benefit.

Jean-Jacques Rousseau's economic and social analysis, carried out about fifty years after Mandeville's, was of a completely different opinion. He delves into the relationship between individuals and society, starting from an assumption contrary to that of Mandeville: the innate benevolence of humanity. He traces the myth of the so-called *bon sauvage* (good savage), who is corrupted once inserted in the collective society. According to the Swiss philosopher, society and private property create social hierarchies and inequalities; humans need a new pact of equality, a social contract between individuals to restore balance and prosperity for all. For Rousseau, it was more important to pursue virtue, real human needs, equality among social classes, and freedom than the wealth of few and the abuses of many. Rousseau was shocked by consumerism too. In the last part of his essay *A Discourse on the Moral Effects of the Arts and Sciences*, he stresses that after the advent of the industrial revolution, new needs emerged among human beings. These needs were not present before, and they were completely superfluous. During consumerism, it is a question of "supply that creates demand," and not the natural vice versa. The availability of new consumer goods fueled the desire to possess them by creating a social and economic paradox: it was no longer produced to consume but to continue to feed a self-strengthening, crazy mechanism.

However, is it possible to create a prosperous and parallelly virtuous society? A collectivity that produces and consumes but not to excess? As Adam Smith said, is it possible to encourage trade and employment without falling into frivolous consumption? At the moment we are in a situation where excessive consumption is leading us to a "planetary ecocide." It is precisely important to analyze consumption behaviors, even of nonbasic goods like art, applying a critical but not reductive perspective. Excessive consumerism, as scholar Gibson (2011) states, is a "collective action problem," "a societal phenomenon," in which different ideas and practices mix. The capitalist ideology that followed the industrial revolution leads us to think that we are at a point of no return for Rousseau's *bon sauvage.* It is important, however, to deal with consumption in its complexity, observing it from the ethical and self-hood point of view but also from that of self-discovery and rational self-interest, without simplistic distortions.

The art market follows the laws of consumption, of stellar prices for highly superfluous goods; it follows the mechanisms of the private opulence of a few individuals. At the same time, it responds to new and higher needs that touch on the spheres of innovation, creativity, and culture and that often benefit the public interest too. One way does not exclude the other. We need to embrace both to reach a complete picture.

Chapter 2:
Art Collectors and the Conspicuous Consumption of the Leisure Class

German collector and curator Wilhelm von Bode stated that art collecting is the noblest of human passions, referring to the cultural nobility and finesse of thought of many art enthusiasts. However, it is necessary to emphasize that art collecting is also an activity that mainly only the most affluent and "noblest" social classes can aspire to. The purchase and circulation of artworks on the market would not be possible without the investments of rich art patrons. However, the consumption of art observes some behavioral peculiarities. The object-art often answers to the higher needs of the buyers; first of all, it attests to their social status. Being able to afford works of art is always a testimony of power, wealth, and taste. It is a way to recognize those belonging to the same social class and to distance themselves from others. To investigate art collecting from a socioeconomic point of view, it is therefore necessary to look at the social stratification that is at the basis of modern society. What happens in the art system often mirrors what is happening at the level of the social class system.

The United States social system has been investigated by the scholar Fussell, who studied the complexity and income inequality of its structure. Fussell (1992) deepens the classic tripartite structure of the upper, middle, and lower class and expands it. According to his analysis, for example, even the upper class has different values and consumption behaviors based on whether wealth is inherited or whether financial success is achieved through work. However, it is the upper class who have the largest amount of economic capital and free time. They tend to fund major art projects and own the largest portion of private art collections. Although the purchase and consumption of art-objects embodies a mythical aura and cultural value, it is not exempt from typical mechanisms of the capitalist economy. Private individuals, as well as banks, companies, and brands, recur to the purchase of artworks for financial investments and tax incentives but also for reasons of status and "washing" of the name compared to competitors. This aspect often highlights intrinsic contradictions in the art world, between those who fund and sponsor art projects and the themes and values that art institutions support.

The ethical short circuit of this funding is often highlighted by artists. For example, we cite Liberate Tate, an art collective that highlights the thirty-year presence of the corporate sponsorship of British Petroleum (BP) in the Tate Modern's projects—projects often dedicated to ecological and environmental issues that have little in common with an oil company. But funding in the field of art is also typical for luxury brands that often associate with museums and artists, highlighting another issue: the ability of visual art to influence consumers' perception of a brand because it is automatically associated with the upper class and prestige (Lee, Chen, and Wang 2015). Museum boards of trustees have also come under scrutiny for funding and ethical issues. Rockefeller is one of the best-known cases. A trustee of the Museum of Modern Art, he was one of the pioneers in the public funding of arts; however, the artists themselves, such as Hans Haacke with his MoMA Poll in the 1970s, have often pointed out to the public that wealth, though used for noble purposes, comes from less than noble backgrounds.

Another recent case is that of Michael Bloomberg, former New York mayor, who was nicknamed Michael the Magnificent by the media in reference to the Renaissance philanthropy of Lorenzo de Medici

(Golway 2010). During his long administration, Bloomberg funded public art projects, such as Christo's and Rondinone's, and invested upward of $3 billion to finance arts and culture in New York City. He is also a relevant private art collector and owns historic artworks from the Hudson River School as well as twentieth-century masterpieces. However, despite this investment in large art institutional projects, his administration was known to ignore problematic issues with education and poverty, thus proving that artistic philanthropy often does not go hand in hand with other political and ethical questions.

However, what philanthropists, brands, and corporations that decide to invest in the art field have in common is that they are part of or primarily target the upper class of society. The upper class is a small slice of society that we can define with the late-nineteenth-century label of the leisure class. This definition is the result of research work realized by the economist and sociologist Thorstein Veblen in 1899, with his *The Theory of the Leisure Class*.

Veblen explored the demand and consumption of the American upper class in terms that were not only strictly economic; he also left space for considerations related to social behavior and lifestyle. This analysis, often satirical, gives relevant insight into attitudes of purchase and human behavior that are also typical of today's art collecting and consumption. According to Veblen, the leisure class was characterized by noninvolvement in productive daily work (considered at the time even shameful) and from the possession of properties and goods. The disposable capital and the "waste" of leisure time (conspicuous leisure) allowed the exponents of the superior class to buy goods through an attitude that Veblen identified as conspicuous consumption (Veblen 1899).

The leisure class decided what to own to display its social status and superiority, and not for functionality or usefulness. Their spending habits were driven by the importance of reputation and by the need to exhibit power, wealth, leisure, and taste (Veblen 1899). Material goods are no longer just objects but real trophies capable of highlighting social differences. Art collecting and the luxury market in general fit into this type of highly symbolic purchasing behavior. Today's leisure class enters the art market because of status symbol issues and because the art-object shows taste and superiority and creates invidious distinction and respect. Exactly as it happened at the time of the Medici family.

It is also important to note the differences of conspicuous consumption in the art system in modern times. Today, mass consumption has led to discrete democratization and accessibility of consumer goods, even luxury ones. Social elites, therefore, can no longer distinguish themselves only through the possession and ostentation of expensive goods, and so other forms of consumption are implemented. Today's leisure class is an aspirational class, which also wants to differentiate itself through culture, taste, experiences such as travel and education, and health. This social elite is interested in the consumer goods themselves but also in how these goods are produced and distributed, for example. Conspicuous consumption is always there, but it is also accompanied by what we might call conspicuous production. The art fits perfectly into this new panorama, which includes not only economic status but also aspirations and lifestyle. An artwork is not the primary product but a by-product capable of representing (and showing off!) the new personal and social values of a modern leisure class.

Chapter 3:
Price and Product: Art as a Veblen Good

In light of this description of the lifestyle of the leisure class, the major purchaser of art, it is difficult to consider an artwork a primary consumer good. But then, do we really need to own art? Where does art fit in the scale of human values?

In 1943, scholar Abraham Maslow wrote a psychology treatise to analyze the hierarchy of human needs. Art ownership is again a terrain that explores multiple domains and human urges. Maslow identified a five-tier model of human needs, often depicted as hierarchical levels of a pyramid. The primary needs, defined by Maslow as deficiency needs, are those that a human being absolutely cannot live without. These physiological needs are food, clothing, care, and safety but also love and belonging. Once these are fulfilled, growth needs take over. These are needs that are not created by the lack of something but rather that are perceived to grow as a person does—desires of esteem, self-worth, and self-actualization (Maslow 1943). Esteem could be for oneself, regarding dignity and independence, but it can also be the urge to feel respected and realized in the eyes of others.

The necessity to own art undoubtedly figures within this desire for prestige and status, involving the sphere of esteem, but not only. Art, referring to Maslow's theoretical model, also touches the level of self-actualization needs. It oscillates between the urge to prove something to others but also to themselves, seeking personal growth and potential through aesthetic experience. In 1970, Maslow made his five-level model more complex by adding cognitive and aesthetic needs. Humans who have largely satisfied the essential needs may feel the desire to surround themselves with beauty, pleasing forms, and balance. Collecting (and especially appreciating) art is one of the best mediums for satisfying this need. Finally, Maslow's hierarchy included another level concerning the possession of the art-object: transcendence needs. According to this new theory, human beings could be motivated by values that transcend the personal self, searching, for example, for mystical, religious, and natural experiences that are often reachable also through art. Human motivation for psychologist Maslow is a sort of dynamic voyage of exploration and change.

It is necessary to underline how this kind of theory is considered by scholars in some ways as classist and one-sided; the human beings who can afford to be self-actualized, personally grown, and able to satisfy and understand needs of transcendence and aesthetics seem to be only those who have already satisfied the very basic physiological needs. Intuitively this may be true, but in reality it assumes that only people who have their basic needs fulfilled can feel desires for growth and fulfillment (Mcleod 2024). This is not so: The leisure and wealthy classes certainly access peak experiences, but even people who have difficulty achieving very basic needs can still feel the urge to grow, to fulfill themselves, to make and own art. Some of them, artists first and foremost, also manage to satisfy it.

On the other hand, there is no denying that the ability to closely observe, to appreciate, and, most of all, to own art is a privilege. Research has shown that differences in social class also influence the perception and evaluation of art (Lareau 2021). Primarily, this gap is due to wealth disparities that allow or disallow the purchase of luxury goods such as artworks. But there is more. The difficulties of getting in touch with the art system do not only concern collecting. Social class disparities are also reflected, for example, in different parenting styles (Lareau 2021), in the access to study, and in the possibility of participating or not in art events. This inequality drastically decreases the possibility of access to tools that allow lower classes to appreciate art and to consider it a relevant need for human fulfillment.

According to Maslow's motivational model, the consumer good "art" is therefore placed among the secondary needs (growth, fulfillment, and transcendence) of the individual. This hierarchical level clearly affects the price of the product. Those who can afford a certain type of leisure market are driven by values that are more aspirational than necessity. Therefore, to pursue these high aspirations, they are willing to pay equally high prices. But there is more. Artworks can be considered actual Veblen products. If we go back to Thorstein Veblen and his *Theory of the Leisure Class*, the scholar highlighted a particular category of goods that apparently contradicted the laws of the market, based on supply and demand. Veblen goods, contrary to the usual, are luxury goods for which the demand increases as the prices increases. They create an economic, paradoxical scenario called the Veblen effect. The price of art follows exactly this counterintuitive law: The higher it is, the more desirable it is, as a status symbol of conspicuous consumption (Bagwell and Bernheim 1966). In some cases, it is precisely the high price that testifies to the value and desirability of the object, as confirmed by the stellar prices of conceptual—even invisible—works of art. In this case, it is the artist's gesture, such as Lucio Fontana's cut or Piero Manzoni's provocations, that elicits the Veblen effect. Art collectors want to pay a higher price because this is the best way to advertise their wealth. In auction houses and galleries, collectors are unlikely to be chasing occasion as, in addition to the investment, the return in terms of status is often more important. Selling a work of art at a cheaper price, in fact, can even damage its image value in the eyes of buyers. The purchase of art is a transaction that acts on a psychological, symbolic, and social level rather than on an economic one.

In this theoretical framework, the purchase behavior of art collectors can be considered invidious consumption, to make the members of other (but also the same) social classes envious of their wealth. But it can also activate what Veblen defined as conspicuous compassion, referring to the ostentatious use of charity, art, and culture funding to enhance the social prestige of the donor.

In conclusion, the importance of the status factor impacts several spheres of the art system. It impacts in economic and practical terms, thus influencing the price of the artwork with the Veblen effect. The higher price becomes the reflection of distinguished identity. It impacts aesthetically and critically, influencing the appreciation of the artwork. The higher the price, the more people are willing to pay for it, to the point that a low price could lead to thinking of an artwork that is not of quality, not of value, not innovative enough. And finally, it impacts the quotations and reputation of the artist. Art collectors often base their opinion of the artists on the monetary value of their artwork. The price of the artwork and the fame of the artist influence each other, in an indissoluble bond.

All of these analyzed components allow us to find different answers to the provocative question posed by scholar Thompson (2010) in his essay on art freakonomics: Why would a smart New York investment banker pay $12 million for the decaying, stuffed carcass of a shark? Why would such a market- and business-informed buyer pay so much to purchase the artwork created by Damien Hirst in 1991, *The Physical Impossibility of Death in the Mind of Someone Living*, that was actually a tiger shark in formaldehyde? Jackson Pollock simply dripped paint onto the canvas, yet his compositions sold for $140 million. Cattelan's golden toilet was estimated at €1.1 million; after the theft, its value rose to €4.5 million. These are astronomical prices that may seem absurd, but they are real. The art system is governed by the laws of the leisure class that are the laws of power: concrete and symbolic. Its vicars, executives of auction houses, and art dealers move this market, intersecting values, strategy, and status consciousness. The modern art market is based on economic and psychosociological assumptions.

In this network of relationships and power holders, it is interesting to conclude by considering those who create (and let go) these mythical products: artists. Often the artist's role and gain in influencing this web of actors are minimal, but this is not always the norm. The case study of Damien Hirst, for example, highlights how artists can create marketing and self-promoting strategies, to the point of being identified as "cultural entrepreneurs" (Enhuber 2014). The scholar Enhuber discussed Hirst's career and entrepreneurial character, showing his artistic, cultural, and commercial approach to art. Hirst achieved success through self-branding and through the industrial production of conceptual art. His practice is parallelly controversial and successful. In fact, one cannot deny the contribution that the artist has made to cultural change, his visionary spirit, and above all the role that he played in changing the East London scene, to the public benefit. Thinking about Hirst, it is impossible to separate the role of the entrepreneur from that of the artist, just as it is difficult to have a dichotomous approach to the wealthy art collectors and funders. The stellar prices of the art world and the art business have an inherent complexity and contradiction. Just as in Mandeville's *Fable of the Bees*, the line between vice and benefit, between hedonism and public interest, is a subtle thread.

Chapter 4:
The Act of Art Collecting

An urgency, an obscure mania, the need to save a series of selected objects from dispersal, from the continuous flux of thought. This is how the Italian writer Italo Calvino described the human impulse to collect in his essays *Collection of Sand*. But if the impetus to collect, archive, and classify objects is as old as humankind, the same cannot be stated for the act of art collecting. Art collecting has a peculiar history and a specific system consisting of distinct strategies, motives, and selecting criteria. Retracing a brief history of art collecting, in its specificity of values, is the scope of this work. The analysis of the historic actors of collecting—exemplary (and not exemplary) art dealers, collectors, and connoisseurs—will guide this research, in the view of explicating a dynamic system of balances and inequalities.

Why deal with the history of art collecting today? In a society where, at first glance, Renaissance patrons, the great papal commissions, noble enthusiasts with the hobby of the *wunderkammer*, no longer exist. Diving into the history of collecting is primarily a social study of art. It therefore allows understanding a currently thriving market and the social and economic values embodied in art possession that are still similar to those of the past. Analyzing the history of collecting involves the mechanisms of art production and sale, with the respective balances of supply and demand and the relationships between art dealers and artists. But it also concerns the fruition of artworks, raising aspects concerning taste and aesthetic evaluation standards. The English art historian Francis Haskell (1976), investigating aspects of taste in art, highlighted how any aesthetic system "is inextricably bound up with a whole series of forces, religious, political, nationalist, economic, intellectual." Reconstructing art collecting history means unraveling the ball of these collective and individual forces—a process where accumulated objects become actual "clues about the past" (Haskell 1976).

Furthermore, looking at the history of collecting is even more relevant today, as collectors' museums created by wealthy patrons are increasingly numerous. The influential list includes the Solomon R. Guggenheim Foundation, the Whitney Museum of American Art, the Frick Collection in New York, the Saatchi Gallery in London, or even the François Pinault and Peggy Guggenheim Foundation in Venice. Social affirmation or a vocation for public education are among the main reasons for collectors' museums, but the interest in donating a personal collection to a wide audience reveals more about these kinds of collectors. It attests that "they are more than collectors, more than critics, they are value creators" (Michelizza 2014). Investigating the history of operating collectors, their taste, and their museums also means understanding their impact on the public museum system. In 2015, there were 216 active private museums, and more than half were created recently (Gnyp 2015). This fact raises questions about the creation of new artistic values that are closely linked to economics, financial opportunities, and inequalities. As Gnyp points out, it can reveal the unwritten rules of a complex network that is experiencing a truly historic shift.

Reasons and Origins: Between Sacred and Profane

The analysis of art collecting history is a timely and urgent issue to move in the current and ever-changing art system. But there are reasons behind collecting that transcend historic periods, which remain unaltered through the centuries. What drives a human being to collect? What motivations prompt them to gather objects? The act of collecting touches both rational and irrational reasons, wealth and mania, sense and feeling. Savvy collectors are informed enthusiasts but also emotionally and economically involved investors. Collected items are in close relationship with them and their system of values, acquiring the status of sacred objects.

I emphasize the term *object* precisely because the particularity of art collecting is the direct fruition of the art object—the interest in possessing original support, and not a reproduction. The impulse to collect art is guided by the strong desire for possession, and not by overconsumption or accumulation. Moreover, it is an act driven by economic, social, and psychological necessities. Baudrillard (1968) underlined how "art collecting rises towards culture"; it contributes to the cultural heritage and is itself a cultural service, particularly through the creation of museums. However, the figure of the collector cannot be mythicized through an *aurea* cultural cover, forgetting also the economic and purely egoistic reasons that underlie the creation of a personal collection. In the civilization of consumption, even the purchase of noble artistic goods is related to the need for self-assertion, status, and profit. As Latin American art collector and author Tiqui Atencio (2016) wittily pointed out in interviewing hundreds of colleagues, some collectors describe their "life-long dedication as a heroic commitment and others as a crazy sickness." Some collectors are more inclined to an "irrational and affective" conduct, whose criteria of selection focus on the uniqueness, quality, and irreplaceability of a mythical object and who perceive the artistic object as closely connected to their identity; there are instead collectors with "rational" conduct, guided by cultural or economic criteria (Poli 2011), who consider authenticity, quality conditions, historic importance, and financial prestige in each acquisition. However, collectors do not collect only for investments, or their collection would lack taste and aesthetic knowledge; they do not look for bargains. According to Iain Robertson (2005), head of art business studies at Sotheby's Institute of Art, "The act of buying and the thrill of the purchase at the right price lies at the bottom behind many a collecting habit." An attitude that well highlights the two souls of art collecting: a balance between awareness of the cultural or historic value and eyes open to the market. Therefore, different values of "money, power, beauty" intersect and circulate among artists, dealers, and collectors (Findlay 2014). Economic, social, and emotional worlds intertwine, creating a complex framework of people and intentions.

In tracing the origins of collecting in the history of humankind, Thomas E. Norton (1980), a prominent art appraiser and former director of Sotheby's, gave us an evocative and significant image: "the creation (and acquisition of noncreators) of art and artifacts is as old as humanity: Ancient Romans collected Greek sculptures, Renaissance Italians collected Roman sculptures, 17th-century monarchs collected Oriental porcelain, 19th-century gentleman collected fossils, butterflies . . . and Renaissance paintings." There is therefore an antique tendency to collect art but above all a circularity of aesthetic sensibilities and taste, which is reflected in the preferred acquisitions of a specific period.

Collecting is rooted in ancient Greece and in the period of classical Rome, where the first collections of sculptures and paintings appeared, as well as scientific collections of precious gems, mainly for decorative purposes. However, already Egyptian, Babylonian, Chinese, and Indian civilizations were collecting precious objects in temples and tombs to glorify sovereigns and deities. Art collecting experienced a factual turning point during the Roman Empire, particularly under the reign of emperors Augustus (27 BC to 14 AD) and Hadrian (117 to 138 AD), with the creation of the first art markets.

However, it is thanks to the Renaissance period that the identity of art collectors, closer to the modern sensibility, begins to develop. Patrons started commissioning artworks from artists to elevate their properties and their social status, to showcase their taste and erudite culture. Furthermore, they provided them with actual resources to deepen their skills, encouraging a climate of experimentation. Parallel to the support for emergent artists, innovative antiquarian culture was raised, linked to the study and possession of antiquities. The Italian families of the Medicis in Florence, the Gonzagas of Mantua, the Montefeltros of Urbino, and the Estes in Ferrara created consolidated art collections, open to the trends of the time and simultaneously of historic importance. In particular, Lorenzo the Magnificent from the Medicis spread the interest for collecting ancient sculptures, showing a possibility of collecting linked to the taste for ruins and a new urge of conservation. Ruins for Renaissance patrons, as Settis (2008) underlined, "told how Rome was great." It represented an actual breakthrough but also with vast symbolic power.

The sixteenth-century collectors, in addition to selection criteria, also questioned how to arrange collections systematically. The cabinets of curiosities, or *wunderkammer*, also known in Italy as *studioli*, were born. In these curious spaces, patrons displayed their artworks and archaeological rarities but also objects and wonders of scientific and natural importance to show an all-around humanistic culture. During the Renaissance, a topical moment for the theorization of art collecting, the concepts exposed before are all evident: the cultural and historic value of the collected objects, the status of collectors and artists, and also the importance of display, of exhibiting the collection in a physical space with sacred connotations, intimate but at the same time conceived as a public legacy. These three focal elements affect all the stakeholders who gravitate to the art collecting system. Art dealers included.

Art Dealers: Portraits of Durand-Ruel, Vollard, and Gimpel from Their Diaries

We explored the many reasons for art collectors and their different behaviors during acquisitions. However, even the figure of the art dealer is not always the same and can assume different postures toward clients and artists. There are traditional or avant-garde dealers: the first interested in consolidating already established artistic trends or artists, the other in affirming new values. There are art dealers who are more tied to the local basin and others who operate at an international level; and there are dealers who have an economic function but also a cultural one, through critical publications, catalogs, and retrospectives.

In this discussion, we will focus on four innovative art dealers, figures who have had in the history of art a leading function in promoting trends and artists who, without their commercial strategies, would be obscured.

The case studies are centered in the early twentieth

century and between the two world wars as well as in the two nerve centers of the art market of the time: Paris and New York. This was done to accurately delineate the differences and similarities of their sales and promotion strategies. Moreover, we chose to use a fascinating tool to get to know them closely: their diaries. The diary is both a literary and a historic document, capable of giving back to the reader a cross section of relationships, places, and intentions.

Looking at the history of the contemporary art market also means looking at Paris at the end of the nineteenth century and the beginning of the twentieth century, where breaking artistic trends were emerging with the Impressionist movement. At the same time, as the aesthetic novelty, a new commercial system was also founded. The Impressionists urgently needed to locate a figure who could materially support their art, and they found this strategist in Durand-Ruel. Paul Durand-Ruel (1931–1922) is the prototype of the innovative art dealer with a clear vision. He published the chronicles of his career, retracing his life from 1831 to 1922, originally in French in 1939 and recently republished in English under the title *Memoirs of the First Impressionist Art Dealer.* His diaries recount his passion and his strenuous defense of young artists such as Manet and Degas, but they also redefine the role of dealers in the art panorama (Durand-Ruel and Durand-Ruel 2014).

Durand-Ruel was not only a friend and patron of the artists but also put in place a well-defined promotion strategy to make successful first the Barbizon school and then the Impressionists. The son of Parisian gallery owners, he inherited the trade but revolutionized its methods. First, Durand-Ruel made sure to promote a type of painting that was not in high demand, in defiance of the quotations. Second, he sought from the beginning to have a monopoly on the artistic current, making exclusive contracts with Impressionist painters. Third, he promoted them on various levels: setting up solo and group exhibitions in his gallery, opening international branches (for example, in New York), and writing about them in specialized magazines—and even founding one, *L'Art dans les Deux Mondes*. This made it a reference point for the international avant-garde, but he was not always successful in his hazardous strategy. According to scholars, the balance of the first Impressionist exhibitions (of which Durand-Ruel had bought huge stocks) was catastrophic: almost five thousand unsold paintings. The decision to open up to the American market transformed his career and was "an intuition that changed the fate of art history and taste" (Benoît 1974). Although Durand-Ruel often risked bankruptcy, critics agree in calling him "one of the most forward-thinking art dealers of all time" and one of the "inventors of Impressionism." Among his most daring business practices was also paying artists a fixed stipend

(Patry 2015). Monet himself, reports the scholar Patry (2015), exalted his essentiality, stating "nous tous, les impressionnistes, lui devons tout." From his diary, we deduce that Durand-Ruel created an unprecedented story: the Impressionists' case. He played a crucial role as a mediator between innovative artists and a hostile public, making them appreciated through methods that are still the same among leading contemporary art dealers.

Another prominent art dealer close to Durand-Ruel, but characterized by a different economic unscrupulousness, is Ambroise Vollard (1866–1939). His attitude is outlined within the pages of his diary, *Recollections of a Picture Dealer* (Vollard 2011). It is a series of reflections about his career as an art dealer but in which he seems to deliberately avoid talking analytically about the artworks and in some passages highlights his vanity. According to scholars, his diary is "a picture of the Paris art scene before World War I, particularly of the less familiar traditional art" (Needham 1978), but the dealer is careful not to share his success secrets with the reader. On the contrary, he romantically presents himself as "a young provincial from La Réunion island in the Indian Ocean, who came to appreciate the best artists of his time" (Needham 1978), artificially deprecating himself. However, the chapters that describe the emergence of his passion for collecting and arts are extremely fascinating. Born in a French colony and surrounded by exoticisms, Vollard spent a lot of time in his drawing room full of native curiosities, "stuffed Bengalis, butterflies in a glass case, shells," as in a real cabinet of curiosities (Vollard 2011). Vollard was also among the greatest promoters of the painter Cézanne, supporting him critically with reviews and studies. He met him once he arrived in Paris: "Paris! The very magic of the name predisposed me to admire everything!" he wrote, beginning to frequent the environment of Montmartre and the artists of the Café de la Nouvelle Athènes (Vollard 2011). Through Vollard and his first solo exhibition in the famous gallery of Rue Lafitte in 1894, Cézanne achieved success. Vollard's shrewd choices as a dealer allowed him to represent a *trait-d'union* between the generation of Impressionists and Postimpressionists up to the avant-garde of Picasso. Like Durand-Ruel, he acquired artworks from innovative artistic currents, accumulating huge stocks of paintings. However, Vollard did not always sign contracts with artists, making successful commercial operations that were often egocentric. His flourishing parallel activity as a publisher of *livres d'artistes* can be interpreted as an initiative to valorize the artists he represented but also, as the scholar Needham (1978) wittily points out, "a way to finally stamp his name on artists' work." This is an example that shows how in the art system, different interests and roles can overlap and unbalance the equilibria.

Another art dealer of the same generation who has left scholars a valuable diary is René Gimpel (1881–1945), a prominent dealer of Jewish descent who died in a concentration camp. Studied in depth by Kostyrko in 2017, Gimpel's is an interwar diary that he kept for twenty-one years that is also rich in sociopolitical testimony and aesthetic analysis. Kostyrko (2017) emphasizes that it is a "sociohistorical document," providing information on both European formulation of taste in fine and decorative arts in the early twentieth century and on the acculturation of American museums. Gimpel was, in fact, of wealthy descent, being the son of Louis Vuitton's niece, and began his career in France as an art dealer specializing in eighteenth-century fine and decorative arts. Nevertheless, he is defined as a transatlantic dealer, as he was among the first to intercept the shift of the art market from Paris to New York. He bought in France but sold to private collectors in North America, enriching what is now the heritage of American museums. His old-European sensibility is often evident in pessimistic anecdotes about immoderate American progress and tycoon collectors.

His point of view, poised between two worlds, gives us a portrait that is "an ethnology of players where the modern art market is a symptom of the modern nation, or a guide to the rules and misrule of consumption" (Kostyrko 2017).

Common traits with the story of René Gimpel (the transatlantic bond, the Jewish descent, the flux between Paris and New York) are also detectable in the story of the Rosenberg brothers. For them, "art dealing was a family affair." Paul Rosenberg (1881–1959) and his brother, Léonce, inherited their father's antique art gallery in 1906 and then devoted themselves to different artists. Paul promoted the French masters of Impressionism and Postimpressionism and then later Picasso, Braque, Léger, and Matisse at an international level, opening branches in London and New York and creating an innovative gallery known as the French Florence. His name as an art dealer is infamous for a case of looting, a truly sensitive issue in the art system. Forced to abandon France during Nazism, Rosenberg was on the list of Jewish art dealers and collectors in Paris. Their avant-garde paintings labeled as "degenerated art" were looted or destroyed by Nazi officials. After World War II, some of the four hundred paintings were returned to their heirs, but others are still lost (Sutton 2019). Paul Rosenberg and the French government worked hard to reconstitute the original nucleus of the picture gallery; as a sign of gratitude, Rosenberg donated thirty-three works to the French museums. His legacy demonstrates the interest of some dealers in making art available to the general public and unites dealers and collectors in a common framework of intentions.

Collectors and Advisers: The Passionate Mission of Personal Museums

When reviewing the history of art collecting and the network that distinguishes it, it is also important to highlight the different modus operandi of collectors. This research focuses on art collectors who then created museum institutions, a choice of economic, cultural, and symbolic impact. Strategic art dealers and sales structures are needed, but in addition to supply, demand must also be investigated. However, some figures work on both fronts: art advisers. These are scholars and art experts who can make their skills available to both galleries and auction houses but who are also consulted by private art collectors. One of the most renowned connoisseurs of art collecting history is Bernard Berenson (1865–1959). The choice of Berenson is not accidental, as the scholar changed the way of looking at and collecting art both for private collections and as an adviser to collectors who founded actual museums. Among the most celebrated experts on the Italian Renaissance, Berenson became indispensable in the recognition and attribution of old masters artworks. According to his biography, his Villa I Tatti in the Florentine countryside, which is now the Harvard Center for Renaissance Studies, became a hub for wealthy collectors, artists, celebrities, and intellectuals (Cohen 2013). Berenson became an authenticator for art dealers like Joseph Duveen but also of art patrons like Assis Chateaubriand; he became the "advisor to nouveau riche gilded age Americans who were building old master collections" (Cohen 2013), and he also sold artworks himself. However, scholars point out that his career was not tension-free, dictated by his scrupulous temperament, strong morals, and Jewishness. Endelman (2014) states how the title of the biography, *A Life in the Picture Trade*, highlights the commercial aspect, the *trading* of artworks that Berenson as a critic perceived as spiritual objects. Berenson was in "an ethical quagmire" in the system of collecting "a moral minefield" that was punctuated by misattributions, fast dealing, and recklessness (Endelman 2014). Berenson perceived the encounter with the work of art not only as professional but also always human and spiritual, a way of exalting one's vitality, and he was "hyper-jealous of paintings" (Bottari 1948). He had a temperament that hardly bowed to the rules of the market. Berenson's story reminds us that the "buying and selling of art, when stripped of its cultural pretensions, is a business like any other business" (Endelman 2014).

Berenson's venture at Villa I Tatti tells us a lot not only about an unquiet art expert but also about collecting in general. His villa was both a private home and also a sort of temple of art. Scholars conceived it like an "oeuvre," where the "value transcends that of the sum of all these individual parts or artworks"; it has a symbolical meaning in its harmonious totality. This spirit of creating a place where the collected artworks are together, but with the goal that it could represent itself as a work of art, where "objects became parts of an organic whole" (Griener 2007), is very common to collectors dedicated to building a personal museum. The idea of amalgamating artworks by criteria of history, aesthetic taste, and cultural association and by providing a cultural service to the community guided, for example, the creation of the multidepartment Museum of Modern Art of New York. Alfred H. Barr (1902–1981), the first MoMA director and who remained so for thirty-eight years, pulled the strings of this immense project. Often accused of "making the history that he had only to document" (Poli 2011), Barr laid the foundations of an intellectual museum, which looked at the intrinsic aesthetics of the art object but also at its techniques and materials (Kantor 2005). As his biography attests, he was a "missionary of the modern," capable of understanding modern art, but also with the *mission* to share it and make it appreciated by the public (Marquis 1989). Barr launched the theoretical framework, but the undertaking of MoMA's collection would not have been possible without the contributions of three visionary female collectors. It all began, states the institutional website, when "three women had a vision." Abby Rockefeller, Lillie P. Bliss, and Mary Quinn Sullivan proposed the idea of creating an institution dedicated to the art of the time and to living artists.

They all were determined art collectors and opponents of academic cultural institutions. Abby Rockefeller was part of the philanthropist family. When the Metropolitan Museum refused her donation of modern art in 1929, she decided to establish an open-minded cultural center, founding the MoMA. Bliss, the daughter of a textile dealer, was one of the most prominent collectors of modern masters in New York. She owned Modigliani, Gauguin, and Monet and donated 150 pieces of her collection to the new museum. Mary Quinn Sullivan, the third cofounder, was a minor collector and later a gallery owner, but with an early career as an art teacher, she promoted the museum in its educational aspects. The trio had a vision, but they also had the resources, planning, and skills to materialize it.

MoMA's mission is configured between private collecting and public vocation, and it also has its criticalities, especially about funding strategies. To learn more just turn your gaze to the world of artists, including those of the Institutional Critique artworks. Famous is Hans Haacke's 1970 MoMA Poll, which investigates the controversial role of major donor and board member Nelson Rockefeller or the 2020 letters of artists protesting against institution unethical ties (News Desk 2020). This is a warning that the art collecting system had and still has its lights and shadows.

Another experience of collecting and creating a personal museum is the adventure of the Museu de Arte de São Paulo (MASP), a private nonprofit institution founded in 1947 by the businessman and arts patron Assis Chateaubriand (1892–1968). Chateaubriand was a prominent figure in the Brazilian media. Founder of the main press chain of Brazil, the Diários Associados group, he was also a politician and far-sighted collector. His intention with the MASP was to create the first collection of modern European and Brazilian art in the southern hemisphere, taking inspiration from Western models but at the same time exhibiting works and artifacts from Europe, Africa, Asia, and the Americas. In this endeavor, as in the case of Berenson, Chateaubriand was guided by the Italian art critic and art adviser Pietro Maria Bardi and his wife, Lina Bo Bardi, the visionary architect who conceived the museum structure. It was a structure that deliberately distanced itself from the traditional layout, envisioned as an "enormous exhibition space, in which [the] visitor was drawn into a jungle of paintings," with a free trajectory. A building that did not want to be a container of art but with a subjective imprint, like that of a collector. Able to tell the "migratory destiny of the pieces, but also to a lack of institutional framings" (Buergel 2011). Lina Bo Bardi's architectural design is no longer visible today and has been replaced, but it tells the story of Chateaubriand's vision. And also, the unscrupulousness of his massive buying campaign, flanked by dealer George Wildenstein, allowed him to acquire masterpieces by old masters from a Europe impoverished by World War II. After all, Chateaubriand said of his strategy as a collector and businessman, "excellency in business means buying *without* money."

Another example that highlights the unethical issues involved in art collecting is the recent case of Swiss collector Emil Georg Bührle (1890–1956). The expansion of the new kunsthalle in Zurich, which displays the collection, highlights the "serious omissions" about the provenance of these artworks. Bührle bought Nazi-looted art, with the fortune made from selling arms to Nazi Germany. When dealing with collecting, independent research is therefore necessary (Hickley 2021). The complexity of the actors involved and their different levels of commitment (economic, cultural, and ethical, above all) must be considered. Visitors of personal museums should be always informed with transparency about the history of the collections and the collectors.

The Great Women of Art Collecting: Gardner, Whitney, Frick, and Guggenheim

A woman was among the first collectors in art history during the Renaissance period. Isabella d'Este, the wife of Francesco Gonzaga, duke of the Italian town of Mantua, exhibited artworks in two spaces of her palace: the *studiolo* and the *grotta*. Women collectors have never stopped showing art to the public, with an often proud and pedagogical spirit. In particular, four American collectors have revolutionized the strategy of personal museums and with different temperaments toward art and artists.

The primary objective of Isabella Stewart Gardner (1840–1924) was to make art accessible. An art collector, philanthropist, and patron, her family wealth came from mining investments. Her collection focused on European and Asian paintings. These masterpieces were frequently chosen during intercontinental trips but also included artworks by contemporaries like Sargent and McNeill Whistler. As a collector, she was advised by the valuable collaboration with the critic Bernard Berenson, who selected Renaissance works for her. The museum Isabella Stewart Gardner created in Boston was basically "her home open to the public," displaying her collection and other personal *mirabilia*. She also worked assiduously on the design of the building, which opened in 1903 with a gallery imitating a fifteenth-century Italian villa. In 2012, the museum boasted an extension designed by the star architect Renzo Piano. Scholars investigated the vision behind the Isabella Stewart Gardner Museum, calling it "the museum of myth" (Chong 2007). This is an extremely personal museum, linked to the taste of its founder. It has "a special appeal to visitors curious about biographies and idiosyncrasies of collectors" (Chong 2007). Gardner was never interested in explicitly explaining the reasons for her collection; her museum's statement concisely reads "for the education and enjoyment of the public forever." For this reason, she always pushed for a spontaneous approach to art. The Gardner Museum was not created as an analytical institution but as a free temple of art, a place where "work of art must live by itself," "where theories were put aside," "a place that would fire emotions and restore life to works of art through domestic intimacy of the setting" (Chong 2007). The Gardner Museum is attractive precisely because of this vision. Its art goes hand in hand with the personality of the mythical woman who collected it, who "rejected intellectualization" in favor of an open-ended atmosphere and a setting of emotion and poetry.

The Whitney Museum of American Art was also founded by a far-sighted collector and already started as a pioneering institution. Besides being a collector and patron, Gertrude Vanderbilt Whitney (1875–1942) was first and foremost an artist herself. Her sculptor's studio in Greenwich Village became first a club and then a gallery, helping young artists who later became established, like Joseph Stella and Edward Hopper. Whitney rejected academicism from within. The history of her museum began when she decided to donate part of her modernist collection to the Metropolitan Museum of Art, but the gift was promptly refused. So, in 1930, she founded her institution, as if it were a parallel, a comparison, the *salon des refuses* of New York art. And it is precisely in the stubborn and contrary spirit of her collection that Whitney's mission was based. The museum's opening announcement stated, "Our present-day productions can be easily seen and compared with others," underlining the desire for confrontation and openness of the American art scene (Burroughs 1932). Whitney considered the other national museums anachronistic, "disconnected from the realities of a networked world," faster and communicative (Anderson 1999). As a sculptor, she was devoted to other artists, her fellows, and, with great modesty, hardly ever exhibited anything of her own. The collection and museum were conceived with the idea of "a nucleus of a museum devoted exclusively to American art" (Force 1943). By American art, she meant creating an institution that embodied the complexity and debates of American society. The Whitney Museum wanted to tell the story of Americans through artists who grasped this connection and who lived in the nation, no matter where they came from.

The temperament of Helen Clay Frick (1888–1984) as a collector was aptly described by her great-granddaughter, who called her "a bittersweet heiress" (Sanger 2008) born in an atmosphere of mournful family events. The monograph provides primary archival material and a truly personal portrait. Frick was one of "the wealthiest unmarried women of America," and she "devoted herself to the preservation and promotion of her father's legacy" (Fahlman 2010). She inherited a familial art collection that flourished with her. Great names such as Turner, Constable, and Vermeer were joined by Rembrandt, Goya, and Monet. Her collection was put on public display in a museum, going from private to public state in 1931. The collector also added an important archive: She established the Frick Art Reference Library. With this institution, the legacy of Helen Frick provides a valuable treasure of bibliographic material for art historians and critics.

One of the most famous collectors is Peggy Guggenheim (1898–1979), who created one of the most important art collections of the twentieth century that can now be visited in Venice. Guggenheim coherently collected Cubist, Surrealist, and Expressionist art but also the art of her friends, such as Picasso, Man Ray, and Dalí, and her lovers, like Ernst and Pollock. Her life as a collector is cataloged in her diary, which reads like a cross between an autobiography and informal memories of rumors, lovers' quarrels, and the stormy art world: *Out of This Century: Confessions of an Art*

Addict (Guggenheim 1980). Guggenheim was highly criticized for her eccentricity and effervescent behavior; even her diary was harshly described as a "relentlessly compulsive recital of her own decadent life," certainly "not the autobiography of an art connoisseur" and more the "confessions of an artist addict" than of a savvy art patron (Altabe 1983). These criticisms overshadow her greatest merit: having promoted with determination and stubbornness a generation of artists who needed attention: the Abstract Expressionists, from Motherwell to Pollock. Peggy Guggenheim "protested revisionism, a bit humorlessly and petulantly, but with reason: she was an important force, and due credit should be given her for determination and initiative" (Rudikoff 1981). The contemporary sensibility of her collection and her self-invention had nothing to envy from her "uncle's garage," as she called the Solomon R. Guggenheim Museum (Guggenheim 1980). Her collection has often been criticized for a kind of laissez-faire attitude: a strong enthusiasm for the discovery, a theatrical display, and a subsequent sloppiness in terms of preservation (Bois 1987). Peggy Guggenheim navigated with a performer's temperament in an era that was the golden age of collecting, when collectors finally opened the doors to their treasures.

Dominique and John de Menil

> "To be controversial means to have original ideas that not everybody has. What's accepted is never what is the most important or the most interesting. To be not controversial is to remain at the lowest common denominator."
>
> —Dominique de Menil (as qtd. in Middleton 2018)

A philanthropist, art collector, and patron, Dominique de Menil was one of the most influential intellectuals in the twentieth-century cultural scene of the United States. Born in 1908 as the daughter of Conrad Schlumberger, a Calvinist Alsatian who made a fortune in the petroleum industry, Dominique Schlumberger was raised in one of the most prominent Protestant families in France (Middleton 2018). Although she and her sisters grew up among intellectuals, scientists, and achievement-oriented businesspeople who held strict Protestant values, the future art collector also had a keen interest in religion and spirituality. Inspired by her father, who was a physics professor, she earned her degrees in mathematics and physics at the Sorbonne. From a young age, Dominique had a passion for collecting curious small objects like fossils, shells, museum notices, stamps, and matchboxes—a passion that would later be reflected in her wunderkamer-style home and in the de Menils' immense art collection (Achenbaum 2009; Middleton 2018). Even in her later years, Dominique kept a special collection in her home, curated specifically for children: a Louis XV cabinet filled with small objects like glass marbles, old coins, antique buttons, tiny perfume bottles, seashells, a pocket watch, an eighteenth-century Persian carving of a fish, and other trinkets (Middleton 2018).

In 1930, Dominique Schlumberger met Jean de Menil, a young Catholic banker from a military family. The couple got married in 1931, and Dominique de Menil decided to convert to French Catholicism the next year, which would deeply influence her perception and understanding of spirituality and modernism. Trying to overcome her family's puritanical understanding of art collecting as immoral and ostentatious, de Menil reconciled traditional conventions and the contradictory impulses of her new faith by finding meanings in artifacts that caught her soulful vision (Achenbaum 2009).

Jean and Dominique de Menil were introduced to modern art by Fr. Marie-Alain Couturier (1897–1954), an unconventional and forward-thinking Dominican priest who held an avant-garde outlook on sacred art and who believed museums of modern art to be places of awe and spiritual meaning:

The priest's moral and aesthetic sensibilities appealed to the de Menils' respect for tradition, penchant for austere clarity, and their desire to make French Catholicism more intellectually vibrant and emotionally vital. So with Fr. Couturier's guidance, the couple turned to novel sources of inspiration, even those—like Modernism—heartily disapproved by Church officials. (Achenbaum 2009)

Dissatisfied with the quality of conventional artworks commissioned by the Catholic Church, Couturier shared with the de Menils his interest in contemporary artistic production and urged them to visit galleries and museums and to start collecting the works of promising artists that spoke to their intuition.

In 1941, the Nazi occupation forced the de Menils to relocate to the United States. They first moved to New York but quickly settled in Houston, Texas, where Jean, now John, would take over the Schlumberger overseas branch (Achenbaum 2009). At the time, Houston had more than one hundred oil fields and thousands of working wells, but it had no active art community, so the de Menils maintained their residences in New York and Paris and made it their mission to bring prominent artists, activists, and intellectuals to their new hometown (Middleton 2018). Designed by architect Philip Johnson, their eclectic family home in River Oaks became a meeting point for people like Max Ernst, René Magritte, Jean-Luc Godard, Henri Cartier-Bresson, Andy Warhol, and many others.

> Thanks to their money and eagerness to contribute to the visual arts, the de Menils quickly made an impact on the community. In the process, as their own understanding of art and spirituality deepened, Jean and Dominique enriched the quality of life in Houston. They offered an urbane blueprint that sometimes was more than other patrons and local institutions could tolerate or would permit. (Achenbaum 2009)

When the de Menils arrived in Houston, the city had one institution of higher education, the Rice Institute, and one museum, the Museum of Fine Arts (Middleton 2018). In 1947, the Basilian Fathers, a French Catholic order, founded the University of Saint Thomas (UST) and invited the de Menils to contribute to the institution's arts department. The couple donated great works of art to UST, bought land to expand the campus, and personally invited influential artists and historians to teach there (Achenbaum 2009). As Dominque noted,

> "[Artists] invite us to celebrate life and to meditate on the mystery of the world, on the mystery of

God. Artists constantly open new horizons and challenge our way of looking at things. They bring us back to the essential." (Middleton 2018)

In 1956, the de Menils recommended Philip Johnson to design the new university campus (James 2010). In 1964, Dominique de Menil became head of UST's art history department, curating many exhibitions assembled from public and private art collections, including works acquired by the de Menils themselves. Apart from the influence of Fr. Marie-Alain Couturier, the de Menils were inspired by the ecumenical teachings of Fr. Yves Congar, who emphasized the laity's role in religion and theology and who advocated for stronger bonds among different religious communities (Achenbaum 2009).

The Basilian Fathers, however, felt that the de Menils' influence was becoming too strong. The collaboration ended in the late 1960s, and the de Menils moved their art department and the works they donated elsewhere (Achenbaum 2009; Middleton 2018).

As Stephen James (2010) put it, the de Menils were more than collectors; they actively commissioned art and architecture to further their vision of the role of art in the community. Their efforts went beyond mere philanthropy and embraced clear social and spiritual goals (James 2010). During the 1950s and 1960s,

Dominique and John de Menil became increasingly involved in the civil rights movement. Houston, known as a breeding ground for oil magnates and millionaires, also had poverty-stricken neighborhoods populated mostly by African American and Latinx communities (Middleton 2018). The de Menils held fundraising events, supported prominent activists and political leaders like Martin Luther King Jr., and personally mentored young activists interested in politics like the future congressman Mickey Leland. In 1960, Dominique de Menil founded an image archive that would be published as the prize-winning four-volume book *The Image of the Black in Western Art* (Achenbaum 2009; James 2010).

Dominique and John de Menil's art collection grew rapidly since they first started acquiring artworks. In 1945, John de Menil bought a 1895 watercolor by Cézanne in New York, and the purchase led the couple to continue collecting pieces from European modernism, and later, works of American Abstract Expressionism, Minimalism, and Pop Art. Influenced by Fr. Couturier's understanding of the intersections between modernism and spirituality, the de Menils were guided by intuition and personal interest, and their eclectic collection eventually became one of the largest private art collections of the twentieth century. Apart from the works of contemporary European and North American artists, they also acquired numerous works of non-Western art and prehistoric art, including Paleolithic bone carvings, Cycladic idols, Byzantine icons, African medieval totems and sculptures, and effigies from Oceania (Middleton 2018).

When the de Menils split from the Basilian Fathers in the late 1960s, they started to imagine a place in Houston where people of all faiths could come together, learn, find peace, and connect on a spiritual level. Their idea came to life in 1971, with the dedication of the Rothko Chapel. Dominique de Menil saw the Abstract Expressionist Mark Rothko as a Jewish prophet, whose large-scale color field paintings dealt with the eternal and ineffable themes of religion, mortality, and death (Achenbaum 2009). As Dominique stated,

> "Like all great artists who follow an inner call, [Rothko] sacrificed everything superfluous to his vision. The message he had to offer was a timeless one. It was a vision of simplicity, a message of silence." (Achenbaum, 2009)

An octagonal building designed by Philip Johnson and paneled with fourteen black canvases by Rothko, the de Menils' chapel was a unique ecumenical center and work of contemporary art where Catholics, Protestants, Jews, Muslims, and Buddhists could come together and conduct liturgies and where Houstonians of all backgrounds could enjoy fine arts, music, literature, film, and public discussions (Achenbaum 2009). According to Dominique de Menil, a conflict existed between Johnson and Rothko, who had different ideas regarding the lighting of the building (de Menil 1971).

Dominique de Menil described the Rothko Chapel as a spiritual environment created by paintings without image, a place where visitors could meditate, find themselves, and go beyond themselves (de Menil, as qtd. in Achenbaum 2009).

> Though each painting is impressive in itself, each derives its full impact from association with the others to which it is subtly related…An octagonal shape seemed appropriate. It facilitated the participation of the audience, encouraged since Vatican II; it pleased Rothko, who had a special liking for the Torcello baptistry and church. (de Menil 1971)

Due to the political context of the time, the Rothko Chapel was also a place where issues of human rights and racial justice were discussed. Barnett Newman's *Broken Obelisk* sculpture, placed in front of the chapel, was dedicated to the memory of Martin Luther King Jr., who was assassinated three years before the chapel's opening. Newman's sculpture was central to a controversy in 1967, because it was originally intended as a gift to the city of Houston, but as the de Menils' grant conditioned that the sculpture be dedicated to the late political leader, it was finally placed on the Menil Foundation's property (Achenbaum 2009).

On the chapel's tenth anniversary, Dominique de Menil established Awards for Commitment to Truth and Freedom (Achenbaum 2009); in 1986, the chapel began sponsoring the Carter-Menil Human Rights Award, established in cooperation with President Jimmy Carter (James 2010).

John de Menil died in 1973, and Dominique de Menil continued developing the Menil Foundation's art collection and philanthropic work. One of her biggest endeavors over the next decade was the development of a museum that would house the de Menil collection and make it accessible to visitors. In the 1980s, Dominique engaged the Italian architect Renzo Piano to design the museum she and her husband had imagined. Her instruction to the architect was to make it small on the outside but big on the inside (Middleton 2018). A modest yet graceful two-story building, the Menil Collection reflected Dominique and John de Menil's vision of a museum as a celebration of the artists. As John de Menil noted, "Art doesn't call for marble floors nor pedestals. It is part of our life, our emotions and our delights. It can be deeply moving but never stuffy" (Middleton 2018).

Housing more than ten thousand works of art, the Menil Collection was officially opened by the seventy-nine-year-old Dominique de Menil on June 4, 1987 (Middleton 2018). The first floor of the museum offered a juxtaposition of large works of contemporary art with artifacts from older, non-Western cultures. Visitors could marvel at a large-scale metal sculpture by John Chamberlain, marble Cycladic idols, alabaster Sumerian statues, Byzantine relics, and paintings by Francis Bacon, Andy Warhol, Yves Klein, Mark Rothko, and Barnett Newman all at once. The collection also included over one hundred paintings and sculptures by Max Ernst; fifty-four paintings and sculptures by René Magritte; Modernist paintings and drawings by Cézanne, van Gogh, Braque, and Picasso; and photographs of Man Ray and Cartier-Bresson.

The second floor of the museum was reserved for what Dominique de Menil called Treasure Rooms: storage spaces for paintings, sculptures, and objects that were not on view in the main gallery spaces. Arranged in salon style, from floor to ceiling, the pieces in the Treasure Rooms were divided by styles and epochs: Modernism, Abstraction, Pop Art, Surrealism, Byzantine icons, and non-Western art from Africa and Oceania (Middleton 2018).

Dominique had managed to create a museum that was as distinctive as its founders. It was filled with their spirit of generosity—first in assembling the collection, then building a home for it, and finally offering it to the public. (Middleton 2018)

Though the Menil Collection was envisioned by both John and Dominique de Menil, the museum deeply reflected Dominique's personal sense of the sacred, the mature spiritual landscape she refined over the last decades of her life (Achenbaum 2009) that combined her inclination for aesthetic simplicity and Protestant modesty, her passion for Byzantine art, and her understanding of art as a force of reconciliation, cultural diversity, and spiritual unity. In 1988, Dominique de Menil commissioned the Byzantine Fresco Chapel, designed by her son, architect Francois de Menil, and officially opened in 1997 next to the Rothko Chapel (Achenbaum 2009).

Over the second half of the twentieth century, the Menil Collection grew into one of the most impressive private art collections in the world, which led them to be considered the Medicis of Modern Art (Glueck 1986). Apart from acquiring works for their own eclectic collection, the de Menils gave generously to other institutions like the Pompidou Center, the MoMA in New York, the Museum of Fine Arts in Houston, and institutions of higher education like the Rice University Art Center and UCT (Middleton 2018). Paintings and drawings from their collection were exhibited at Brandeis University, the University of California at Berkeley, the Museum of Art, Rhode Island School of Design, and many museums around Europe (de Menil 1973). Dominique de Menil served as director of the Institute for the Arts at Rice University, curating major exhibitions, organizing lectures, and developing arts publications.

Through all the art collecting, swirl of activities, and commitments to global causes, Dominique de Menil's spirituality illuminated the landscape, animating all that she did, everything she accomplished . . . in the face of silence, she also grew in experience and wisdom with the passage of time. (Achenbaum 2009)

Chapter 5:
Contemporary Trends and New Paths: The Art Basel and UBS Global Art Market Reports

The Art Market Report is a comprehensive analysis of the global art market published by Art Basel and UBS annually. Since 2017, Dr. Clare McAndrew, cultural economist and founder of Arts Economics, has been providing key insights into important trends and trajectories in the arts market, analyzing sales and obtaining projects from different actors in the field—from galleries, auction houses, and art fairs to dealers and collectors. The latest edition, published in March 2024, provides an overview of trends in the world art market during the previous year, marked by political and economic uncertainties.

2023 Fine Arts Market Sales Decreased in Value but Not in Volume

According to the Art Market Report 2024, global sales in 2023 were down by 4 percent, with total sales estimated around $65 billion. While total sales dropped compared to previous years, values remained above the prepandemic level of $64.4 billion in 2019. Whereas the top end of the market saw a slowing of growth, the volume of transactions grew by 4 percent compared to 2022, increasing to 39.4 million thanks to transactions at lower price levels.

Non-Fungible Token Sales Decline Significantly

Non-fungible token (NFT) sales decreased in 2023 by 7 percent in auctions and by 3 percent in dealer sales while private sales in auction houses increased by 2 percent compared to 2022. A 7 percent rise was reached in online sales, with total sales estimated around $11.8 billion, which was double the amount of prepandemic years and accounted for 18 percent of the total turnover in the global market. Around 48 percent of dealers surveyed for the report expect the online market to keep growing, as opposed to 7 percent who expect a decline in online sales. More than 95 percent of online-only transactions were for sales valued at less than $50,000—sales of art pieces with the highest prices remained predominantly offline. Sales on NFT platforms declined by 51 percent, reaching $1.2 billion in 2023, compared to the $2.9 billion peak in 2021.

A Postpandemic Rebound in the Chinese Arts Market

The four biggest markets in 2023 were the US, China, the UK, and France, respectively. The US market accounted for 42 percent of global sales by value, which was a 3 percent drop compared to the previous year. Mainland China and Hong Kong became the world's second largest market, surpassing the UK, with its share rising to 19 percent. After reaching a record high of $30.2 billion in 2022, the US market declined to $27.2 billion in 2023; however, it still remained the global center of high-end auction sales.[1]

Digital Art Declines in Value amid Economic Uncertainty

As Clare McAndrew points out, the year 2023 was marked by an elevated degree of uncertainty and risk aversion, which is part of the reason why 86 percent of dealer sales by value were anchored in traditional media like sculpture and painting, a 2 percent rise compared to 2022. On the other hand, slides of digital works and video art declined by 5 percent, accounting for under 1

---

1   The Art Basel and the UBS Global Art Market Report use the following three categories of price ranges to track sales in the arts market: (1) the low-end segment: works sold for up to $50,000; (2) the middle market: price segments ranging from $50,000 to $250,000 and from $250,000 to $1 million; and (3) the high-end segment: prices in excess of $1 million, including ultra-high end, with prices over $10 million.

percent of total dealer sales. The largest share of sales by value in 2023, 44 percent, was held by transactions made in person. Direct sales by galleries rose to 64 percent in 2023, compared to 48 percent in 2019.

Public auction sales saw a decline of 7 percent, coming down to $25.1 billion in 2023. The biggest decline was in transactions of pieces valued over $10 million while sales in midrange and lower-priced segments continued to grow:

> After being the fastest-growing segment in 2021 and 2022, it had the lowest growth of all in 2023, as the number of lots surpassing $10 million sold at auction fell by 25% and values decreased by 40% year-on-year, versus low, positive growth in the market under $50,000. (The Art Market Report 2024)

Despite the decline in sales within the $10 million-plus segment, it is still one of the fastest-growing segments of the market, rising by 380 percent since 2009. Taking inflation into account, the high-price end of the global art market has grown 2.5 times its size.

Total sales by auction companies were down by 5 percent compared to 2022 but above pre-pandemic levels, nevertheless. The US, China (Mainland China and Hong Kong), and the UK were the largest auction markets in 2023, making up 74 percent of public auction sales by value.

2023 Art Market Trends by Sector

To analyze trends in different sectors within the fine arts market, the Art Market Report uses the following categories: (1) postwar and contemporary art, defined as the works of artists born after 1910 and 1945, respectively, with living artists as a subset of this sector; (2) modern art, defined as artists born between 1875 and 1910; (3) Impressionist and Postimpressionist art, defined as artists born between 1821 and 1874; and (4) old masters, referring to artists born between 1250 and 1821 and to European old masters as a subset of the old masters segment.

Postwar and Contemporary Art

In 2023, postwar and contemporary art was the largest sector in the fine art auction market, holding 53 percent of global sales value and 55 percent of sales volume (the older postwar subsector accounted for 66 percent of sales by value). Sales in this sector dropped by 16 percent compared to 2022, reaching $6.5 billion, making 2023 the second year of a decline in sales. Both contemporary and postwar art saw a decline in value, however, with sales falling to $2.2 billion and $4.3 billion, respectively. Nine of the top twenty lots in this sector were sold in China, making it a considerable location on the market, along with New York.

New works made up one-third of the lots sold for more than $1 million in the postwar and contemporary sector. Among the most highly priced new works sold at auction in 2023 were Cui Ruzhuo's 2019-piece *Rafting in Wind and Rain* sold at Beijing Yongle Auction Company for $33.1 million, Cy Twombly's *Untitled (Bacchus 1st Version II)* from 2004 sold at Christie's for $20 million, and David Hockney's *Early Blossom, Woldgate* (2009) sold for $19.4 million, also at Christie's.

The highest-selling artist at auction in the postwar and contemporary art sector in 2023 was Gerhard Richter. Although down by 5 percent compared to the previous year, Richter's works were sold at auction for a total of $252 million. The second highest-selling author was Jean-Michel Basquiat, whose works sold for $238 million, increasing by 7 percent compared to 2022. Consistently in the top twenty ranking artists both by number of exhibitions and by price ranges, Andy Warhol fell from first to third place between 2022 and 2023, with sales declining from $570 million to $191 million in just one year.

Female Artists on the Rise in 2023

Yayoi Kusama and Joan Mitchell were among the

top five highest selling artists in 2023, indicating a slow increase in the representation of female artists in the global arts market. Although the total share of female artists represented by galleries increased by only 1 percent in 2023, a substantial shift can be seen by comparing the share of female artists in the primary arts market in 2018 (36 percent) and 2023 (46 percent).

Interestingly, high net worth collectors tended to have a larger share of female artists' works in their collections (54 percent). In addition, a positive link between gender representation and the performance of galleries can be noticed in both 2022 and 2023, as galleries with fewer than 50 percent of female artists had a 4 percent drop in sales in 2023, and galleries with more than 80 percent of female artists had a 20 percent rise in sales in 2022. Still, galleries with a yearly turnover of over $10 million were shown to have only 35 percent of female artists in their collections.

Modern Art Sector

The modern art sector accounted for 24 percent of fine art auction sales in 2023 but fell below 2019 levels with $3 billion in sales. Pablo Picasso was the highest-selling artist in this sector and overall, for the sixth year in a row, with sales of $603 million. Picasso's *Femme a la Montre* (1932) sold for $139 million at Sotheby's in New

York, making it the highest price overall at auction in 2023, while the second place was held by his 1934-piece *Femme Endormie*, which sold for $42.9 million at Christie's. Apart from Picasso, the top five artists in the modern art sector were Zhang Daqian, René Magritte, Fu Baoshi, and Marc Chagall, comprising 42 percent of the sector's value.

Impressionist and Postimpressionist

The Impressionist and Postimpressionist sector, which saw a 160 percent rise in value in 2022, dropped from $2.6 billion to $1.7 billion. Works priced over $1 million accounted for 60 percent of the sector's total sales, and 15 works sold for more than $10 million, compared to 31 works in 2022. The Chinese painter Qi Baishi was the highest-selling artist in this sector in 2023, with sales of $217 million.

Claude Monet's works sold for a total of $195 million, moving him to second place among the top five artists in the Impressionist and Postimpressionist category. Monet's 1917 piece *Le Bassin aux Nymphéas* sold for $74 million at Christie's, which is one of the highest prices ever achieved at auction for the artist. At Sotheby's, Claude Monet's *Peupliers au Bord de l'Epte, Temps Couvert* from 1891 sold for $30.8 million.

Gustav Klimt, Paul Cézanne, and Vasily Kandinsky, followed Qi Baishi and Cézanne in the top five, accounted for 43 percent of the sector's entire value in 2023. Gustav Klimt's 1901-piece *Insel im Attersee* sold for $53.2 million at Sotheby's while Paul Cézanne's *Fruits et Pot de Gingembre* (1890–1893) reached $38.9 million at Christie's. According to McAndrew, however, the Impressionist and Postimpressionist sector saw a significant decline in high-value lots. The number of works in this sector selling in the US market for above $1 million fell by 28 percent while ultrahigh-end lots selling for more than $10 million dropped from 23 in 2022 to 10 in 2023.

Old Masters

The old masters segment saw a 15 percent rise in value, due in large part to a recovery of the Chinese art market, but still remained below prepandemic levels. The European old masters subsector declined by 17 percent, with a total of $481 million, which is above 2019 levels but well below sales in the previous decade. Overall sales dropped by 3 percent in volume, and only six works sold for more than $10 million. Two of the highest prices achieved were both for works by Flemish artist Peter Paul Rubens: his 1609 painting *Salome Presented with the Head of Saint John the Baptist* sold for $26.9 million, and his 1620-piece *Portrait of a Man as Mars* reached

$26.2 million. Both sold at Sotheby's. These two Rubens works ranked in the artist's top five highest-ever prices but still well under the record-breaking $76.7 million reached in 2002 for *The Massacre of the Innocents* (c. 1608–1609). Altogether, the European old masters sector fell behind compared to 2021 and 2022, when Sandro Botticelli's *Portrait of a Young Man Holding a Roundel* (c. 1480) was sold for $92.2 million at Sotheby's.

Outlooks for Collecting in Upcoming Years

Despite a decline in sales across sectors, the global arts market is still recovering from the long-term economic effects of the COVID-19 pandemic, which is why many actors remain optimistic about the outlooks for 2024. Around 36 percent of dealers reported expecting an improvement in sales in the next year while 48 percent expect sales to remain the same. The largest dealers, with turnover of greater than $10 million, were the most hopeful in 2023, with 54 percent of them projecting a rise in sales. In the auction sector, 38 percent of mid-tier businesses expect sales to improve in 2024 while only 4 percent predict a decline in their own sales.

In the post pandemic world, online sales in the arts market seem to be on a continual upturn. Considering shifting economic circumstances, investments in traditional media like painting, sculpture, and works on paper seem to carry less risk than digital artworks, film, and video. Despite a short-lived surge in sales of digital artworks that occurred with the emergence of art-related NFTs, the bubble seems to have burst, as NFT sales are declining rapidly.

The number of female artists represented by galleries with lower annual turnovers is on the rise, but higher equality and diversity in representation seem to be positively correlated with gallery success rates. High-end sales of works by female artists are also growing in prominence, signifying great potential in investing in women's artistic practices. Emerging markets, dealers, galleries, and auction houses in East Asia are becoming more influential as the Chinese market moves up the ladder, replacing the UK as the second largest arts market in the world.

Between 2016 and 2023, changes in trends in the global arts market have been slow when it comes to diversity and representation. The highest-ranking artists based on the number of sales, representation in high-end galleries, and values of individual lots in the postwar and contemporary art sector, including living artists, have overwhelmingly been white male artists coming from the Global North. Since the publication of the first Art Basel and UBS reports, the artists dominating the global arts market have been Gerhard Richter, Andy Warhol,

David Hockney, Cy Twombly, and Roy Lichtenstein. With the exception of Zao Wou-Ki, Wu Guangzhong, and Cui Ruzhuo, who have made the top five and the top twenty ranks thanks to the growing influence of the Chinese market, the highest-ranking artists consistently come from the US and the UK; this is likely to continue in the upcoming years, considering that these countries represent the largest art markets. In 2021, for example, 75 percent of the highest-value lots sold within the postwar and contemporary sector were at Christie's and Sotheby's.

Despite a general lack of diversity, women artists have slowly become more present in the arts market, both in high-end galleries and auctions and in midrange and low-end sectors. The share of female artists represented by galleries has been on a slow rise, from 33 percent in 2018 to 37 percent in 2019, 39 percent in 2020, and 40 percent in 2021. Yayoi Kusama, Joan Mitchell, and Louise Bourgeois have been among the top twenty highest-ranking female artists between 2016 and 2023, with Kusama being one of the top-selling living artists in 2022 (along with Gerhard Richter and David Hockney). One trend that is still significant despite the slow increase in gender representation is that women artists represented by galleries tend to be young emerging artists rather than midcareer and established female artists.

Regarding different media, painting has consistently been the most prominent form on the arts market, followed by sculpture and works on paper. Among the most valuable lots in the postwar and contemporary sector, Abstract Expressionism (Jackson Pollock, Willem de Kooning, Cy Twombly), color field painting (Mark Rothko), and Pop Art (Andy Warhol, David Hockney) have dominated, followed by conceptual art and sculpture in the expanded field (Jeff Koons, Louise Bourgeois). Immersive and digital art are, however, becoming increasingly influential.

Although major changes are unlikely to occur in the global arts market in upcoming years, the existing trends seem to point toward greater diversity in the future. Increased online sales and the expansion of markets outside the US and Europe indicate the possibility of greater visibility for artists from marginalized communities, including women, indigenous, Black, and Latinx artists. One major driver of positive change has been specific art collectors who have helped shape the global arts market through their patronage of emerging artists and a keen sense of foresight.

One of the most significant contributors to greater diversity and inclusivity in the art world was the collector and philanthropist Susan and Michael Hort. The Horts' vision for their art collection is to actively seek out artists from diverse backgrounds and underrepresented communities, providing them with opportunities for recognition and support and challenging traditional power structures within the arts.

Another prominent figure who pushed boundaries in collecting, advocacy, and patronage in the global arts market is Beth Rudin DeWoody. DeWoody is a vocal advocate for women artists and underrepresented voices within the art world. She actively seeks out and collects works by female artists, artists of color, and LGBTQ+ artists, helping to amplify their voices and increase their visibility within the arts community. Her collection, on view at the Bunker Artspace since 2017, includes works by Kara Walker, Guerilla Girls, Niki de Saint Phalle, Kehinde Wiley, Sanford Biggers, and many others.

Along with Beth DeWoody and Susan and Michael Hort, Don and Mera Rubell have made significant contributions to the arts market through their passionate engagement with contemporary art, a pioneering approach to collecting, and the establishment of the Rubell Museum, a renowned private art collection and cultural institution. The Rubell family began collecting art in the 1960s, focusing on emerging artists and showing a keen eye for spotting rising talents. In 1993, the Rubell Family Collection was established, and it soon became one of the largest privately owned contemporary art collections in the world. Apart from championing young and emerging artists from diverse backgrounds, the Rubells have always shown a great commitment to accessibility, arts mediation, audience development, and the democratization of contemporary art.

Although changes in the art world are slow and there is still a lot of room for improvement when it comes to a lack of diversity, openness to emerging artists, and innovative art forms and media, the legacies of prominent collectors and the positioning of a few individual artists in the global market show that progress can be made when different actors are willing to take risks and push boundaries.

Bibliography:

Achenbaum, Andrew W. 2009. "The Spiritual Landscapes of Dominique de Menil." *Journal of Religion, Spirituality, & Aging* 21 (3): 145–58. https://doi.org/10.1080/15528030902803863.

Altabe, Joan B. 1983. Review of *Out of This Century: Confessions of an Art Addict*, by Peggy Guggenheim. *Leonardo* 16 (2): 157. https://doi.org/10.2307/1574836.

Anderson, Maxwell L. 1999. "Notes on the Mission of the Whitney Museum of American Art." *American Art* 13 (2), 84–86. www.jstor.org/stable/3109301.

Atencio, Tiqui. 2016. *Could Have, Would Have, Should Have: Inside the World of the Art Collector*. New York: Artbook.

Bagwell, Laurie Simon, and B. Douglas Bernheim. 1996. "Veblen Effects in a Theory of Conspicuous

Consumption." *The American Economic Review* 86 (3): 349–73. www.jstor.org/stable/2118201.

Baudrillard, Jean. 1968. *Le Système des Objets*. Paris: Gallimard.

Benoît, Gérard. 1974. "Durand-Ruel." *Esprit* 433 (3): 489–90. www.jstor.org/stable/24262948.

Bois, Yve-Alain. 1987. Review of *Peggy Guggenheim Collection, Venice*, by Angelica Z. Rudenstine. *The Art Bulletin* 69 (3): 481–85. https://doi.org/10.2307/3051075.

Bottari, Stefano. 1948. "Bernard Berenson." *Belfagor* 3 (6): 684–88. www.jstor.org/stable/26047378.

Buergel, Roger M. 2011. "'This Exhibition Is an Accusation': The Grammar of Display According to Lina Bo Bardi." *Afterall: A Journal of Art, Context and Enquiry* 26: 51–57. https://doi.org/10.1086/659295.

Burroughs, Bryson. 1932. "The Whitney Museum of American Art." *The Metropolitan Museum of Art Bulletin* 27 (2): 42–44. https://doi.org/10.2307/3255255.

Chalk, Alfred F. 1966. "Mandeville's *Fable of the Bees*: A Reappraisal." *Southern Economic Journal* 33 (1): 1–16. https://doi.org/10.2307/1055985.

Chong, Alan. 2007. "Mrs. Gardner's Museum of Myth." *RES: Anthropology and Aesthetics* 52: 212–20. www. jstor.org/stable/20167756.

Cohen, Rachel. 2013. *Bernard Berenson: A Life in the Picture Trade*. New Haven, CT: Yale University Press.

de Menil, Dominique. 1971. "The Rothko Chapel." *Art Journal* 30 (3): 249–51.

Dufrenne, Mikel. 1965. "Existentialism and Existentialisms." *Philosophy and Phenomenological Research* 26 (1): 51–62. https://doi.org/10.2307/2105468.

Durand-Ruel, Flavie, and Paul Durand-Ruel. 2014. *Paul Durand-Ruel: Memoir of the First Impressionist Art Dealer (1831–1922)*. Paris: Flammarion.

Endelman, Todd M. 2014. Review of *Bernard Berenson: A Life in the Picture Trade*, by Rachel Cohen. *AJS Review* 38 (2): 487–89. www.jstor.org/stable/24273674.

Enhuber, Marisa. 2014. "How Is Damien Hirst a Cultural Entrepreneur?" *Artivate* 3 (2): 3–20. www.jstor.org/stable/10.34053/artivate.3.2.0003.

Fahlman, Betsy. 2010. Review of *Helen Clay Frick: Bittersweet Heiress*, by Martha Frick Symington Sanger. *Woman's Art Journal* 31 (1): 52–53. www.jstor.org/stable/40605244.

Findlay, Michael. 2014. *The Value of Art: Money, Power, Beauty.* Revised ed. New York: Prestel USA.

Force, Juliana. 1943. *Memorial Exhibition: Gertrude Vanderbilt Whitney.* New York: Whitney Museum of American Art.

Fussell, Paul. 1992. *Class: A Guide through the American Status System*. New York: Touchstone.

Gibson, Andrew. 2011. "Ideas and Practices in the Critique of Consumerism." *Environmental Philosophy* 8 (2): 171–88. www.jstor.org/stable/26168078.

Gimpel, René. 1966. *Diary of an Art Dealer*. New York: Farrar, Straus & Giroux.

Glueck, Grace. 1986. "The de Menil Family: The Medici of Modern Art." *New York Times*, May 18, 1986. www.nytimes.com/1986/05/18/magazine/the-de-menil-family-the-medici-of-modern-art.html.

Gnyp, Marta. 2015. *The Shift: Art and the Rise to Power of Contemporary Collectors*. Stockholm: Art and Theory.

Golway, Terry. 2010. "Michael Bloomberg, Temporary Savior of the Arts." Politico. June 2, 2010. www.politico.com/states/new-york/albany/story/2010/06/michael-bloomberg-temporary-savior-of-the-arts-000000.

Griener, Pascal. 2007. "The Collector's Art Museum as a Symbolic Body." *RES: Anthropology and Aesthetics* 52: 190–97. www.jstor.org/stable/20167754.

Guggenheim, Peggy. 1980. *Out of This Century: Confessions of an Art Addict.* New York: Anchor Books.

Haskell, Francis. 1976. *Rediscoveries in Art: Some Aspects of Taste, Fashion, and Collecting in England and France.* Ithaca, NY: Cornell University Press.

Honig, Elizabeth Alice. 1998. "Making Sense of Things: On the Motives of Dutch Still Life." *RES: Anthropology and Aesthetics* 34: 166–83. www.jstor.org/stable/20140414.

James, Stephen. 2010. "The Menil Connection: Louis Kahn and the Rice University Art Center." *Journal of the Society of Architectural Historians* 69 (4): 556–77. https://doi.org/10.1524/jsah.2010.69.4.556.

Kantor, Sybil Gordon. 2005. Review of *Alfred H. Barr, Jr. and the Intellectual Origins of the Museum of Modern Art. History of Education Quarterly* 45 (4): 656–58. https://doi.org/10.1017/s0018268000040498.

Kostyrko, Diana J. 2015. "René Gimpel's *Diary of an Art Dealer." Burlington Magazine* 157 (1350).

Kostyrko, Diana J. 2017. *The Journal of a Transatlantic Art Dealer: René Gimpel 1918–1939*. Bilingual ed. Turnhout, Belgium: Brepols.

Kottasz, Rita, Roger Bennett, Sharmila Savani, Wendy Mousley, and Rehnuma Ali-Choudhury. 2007. "The Role of the Corporate Art Collection in Corporate Identity Management: The Case of Deutsche Bank." *International Journal of Arts Management* 10 (1): 19–31. www.jstor.org/stable/41064905.

Lareau, Annette. 2021. *Unequal Childhoods: Class, Race, and Family Life*. Oakland: University of California Press.

Lee, Hsiao-Ching, Wei-Wei Chen, and Chih-Wei Wang. 2015. "The Role of Visual Art in Enhancing Perceived Prestige of Luxury Brands." *Marketing Letters* 26 (4): 593–606. www.jstor.org/stable/24571618.

Marquis, Alice Goldfarb. 1989. *Alfred H. Barr, Jr: Missionary for the Modern*. Chicago: Contemporary Books.

Maslow, Abraham. 1943. "A Theory of Human Motivation." *Psychological Review* 50 (4): 370–96. https://doi.org/10.1037/h0054346.

Maslow, Abraham. 1970. *Motivation and Personality.*

2nd ed. New York: Harper & Row.

Mcleod, Saul. 2024. "Maslow's Hierarchy of Needs." Simply Psychology. January 24, 2024. www. simplypsychology.org/maslow.html.

Michelizza, C. 2014. "Describe the Role of Collectors in the XXI Century, in Terms of Effects on the Art Market, Influence on Artistic Creation, Diffusion and Knowledge of Artists and Artworks." *The Tafter Journal*.

Middleton, William. 2018. *Double Vision: The Unerring Eye of Art World Avatars Dominique and John de Menil*. New York: Knopf.

Needham, Gerald. 1978. Review of *Recollections of a Picture Dealer*, by Ambroise Vollard. *RACAR: Revue d'art Canadienne / Canadian Art Review* 5 (2): 149. www.jstor.org/stable/42630177.

News Desk. 2020. "Artists Pen Letter Protesting MoMA's Ties to Controversial Donors." Artforum. January 14, 2020. www.artforum.com/news/ artists-pen-letter-protesting-momas-ties-to-controversial-donors-246089.

Norton, Thomas E. 1980. "Art Collecting: Avocation or Aberration?" *American Bar Association Journal* 66 (11): 1392–95. www.jstor.org/stable/20746830.

Patry, Sylvie, ed. 2015. *Inventing Impressionism: Paul Durand-Ruel and the Modern Art Market*. London: National Gallery.

Poli, Francesco. 2011. *Il Sistema Dell'Arte Contemporanea: Produzione Artistica, Mercato, Musei*. Rome: Editori Laterza.

Robertson, Iain. 2005. *Understanding International Art Markets and Management*. New York: Routledge.

Rosenberg, Nathan. 1963. "Mandeville and Laissez-Faire." *Journal of the History of Ideas* 24 (2): 183–96. https://doi.org/10.2307/2707844.

Rudikoff, Sonya. 1981. Review of *Out of This Century: Confessions of an Art Addict*, by Peggy Guggenheim. *The American Scholar* 50 (1): 136–41. www.jstor.org/stable/41210709.

Sanger, Martha Frick Symington. 2008. *Helen Clay Frick: Bittersweet Heiress*. Pittsburgh: University of Pittsburgh Press.

Settis, Salvatore. 2008. "Collecting Ancient Sculpture: The Beginnings." *Studies in the History of Art* 70: 12–31. www.jstor.org/stable/42622671.

Sutton, Benjamin. 2019. "The Famed Jewish Art Dealer

Who Fought to Retrieve 400 Stolen Works from the Nazis." Artsy. January 14, 2019. www.artsy.net/article/ artsy-editorial-famed-jewish-art-dealer-fought-retrieve-400-stolen-works-nazis.

Thompson, Don. 2010. *The $12 Million Stuffed Shark: The Curious Economics of Contemporary Art*. New York: St. Martin's Griffin.

Veblen, Thorstein. 1899. *The Theory of the Leisure Class*. Reprint, 1994. New York: Dover.

Vollard, Ambroise. 2011. *Recollections of a Picture Dealer*. New York: Dover.

Sitography

"The Benefactor." 1998. *The New Yorker*, June 8, 1998. www.newyorker.com/magazine/1998/06/08/the-benefactor.

Cohen, Alina. 2018. "10 Remarkable Revelations from a New Biography on Trailblazing Art Patrons John and Dominique de Menil." Artnet. April 2, 2018. https:// news.artnet.com/art-world/10-surprising-revelations-biography-de-menil-1257254.

Hickley, Catherine. 2021. "An Arms Dealer Casts a Shadow over Kunsthaus Zurich." *The Art Newspaper*, January 27,

2021. www.theartnewspaper.com/2021/01/27/an-arms-dealer-casts-a-shadow-over-kunsthaus-zurich.

Lesser, Casey. 2018. "5 Collecting Lessons from Dominique and John de Menil." Artsy. April 18, 2018. www.artsy.net/article/artsy-editorial-5-collecting-lessons-dominique-john-de-menil.

The Menil Collection. n.d. "History." Accessed February 7, 2024. www.menil.org/about/history.

Metropolitan Museum of Art Libraries. n.d. "The John and Dominique de Menil Collection." Accessed February 27, 2024. https://libmma.contentdm.oclc.org/digital/collection/p16028coll15/id/3627.

Middleton, William. 2018a. "The High Society Love Story behind Dominique and John de Menil's Legendary Art Collection." *W* Magazine, March 7, 2018. www.wmagazine.com/story/dominique-john-de-menil-art-collection.

Middleton, William. 2018b. "The de Menil Family Raised Good Taste to an Art Form." *Town & Country*, November 2, 2018. www.townandcountrymag.com/leisure/arts-and-culture/a18929606/de-menil-family-collection.

Museu de Arte de São Paulo. n.d. "About MASP."

Accessed April 10, 2024. https://masp.org.br/en/about, retrieved 5/11/2021.

Museum of Modern Art. n.d.-a. "Starting (a Collection) from Scratch: MoMA through Time." Accessed May 11, 2021.   www.moma.org/interactives/moma_through_time/1920/starting-a-collection-from-scratch.

Museum of Modern Art. n.d.-b. "Three Women Have a Vision: MoMA through Time." Accessed May 11, 2021.   www.moma.org/interactives/moma_through_time/1920/three-women-have-a-vision.

Russell, John. 1998. "Dominique de Menil, 89, Dies; Collector and Philanthropist." *New York Times*, January 1, 1998. www.nytimes.com/1998/01/01/arts/dominique-de-menil-89-dies-collector-and-philanthropist.html.

The Art Basel and UBS Global Art Market Report

The Art Basel and UBS Global Art Market Report 2017:

https://theartmarket.artbasel.com/previous-reports

The Art Basel and UBS Global Art Market Report 2018:

https://theartmarket.artbasel.com/previous-reports

The Art Basel and UBS Global Art Market Report 2019:

https://theartmarket.artbasel.com/previous-reports

The Art Basel and UBS Global Art Market Report 2020:

https://theartmarket.artbasel.com/previous-reports

The Art Basel and UBS Global Art Market Report 2021:

https://theartmarket.artbasel.com/previous-reports

The Art Basel and UBS Global Art Market Report 2022:

https://theartmarket.artbasel.com/previous-reports

The Art Basel and UBS Global Art Market Report 2023:

https://theartmarket.artbasel.com/previous-reports

The Art Basel and UBS Global Art Market Report 2024:

www.ubs.com/global/en/our-firm/art/collecting/art-market-survey.html

www.ingramcontent.com/pod-product-compliance
Lightning Source LLC
Chambersburg PA
CBHW041248030626
46017CB00009B/224